Fundamental Solos for MALLETS

11 Early- to Late-Intermediate Solos for the Developing Mallet Player

MITCHELL PETERS

Table of Contents

Foreword

The following solos were written as a companion to *Fundamental Method for Mallets* with the developing mallet player in mind, but can act as supplementary material to the simultaneous study of any method book.

The intent of these pieces is to provide musical material which will give the progressing student a chance to put to practical use his or her developing technical skills. In addition, any of the following solos may be used as either contest or jury pieces.

Finally, it is the author's hope that these studies will be fun for the students to play.

Copyright © MCMXCIX by Alfred Publishing Co., Inc.

All rights reserved. Printed in USA.

ISBN: 0-7390-0621-5

Cover photograph: Courtesy of Yamaha Corporation of America

Modo Nuovo

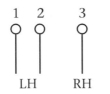

Deserted Road

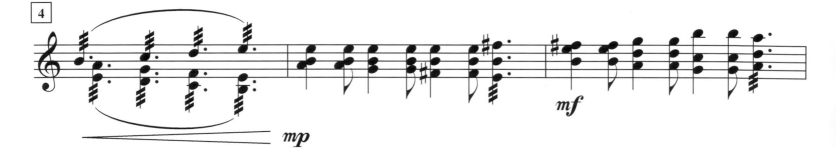

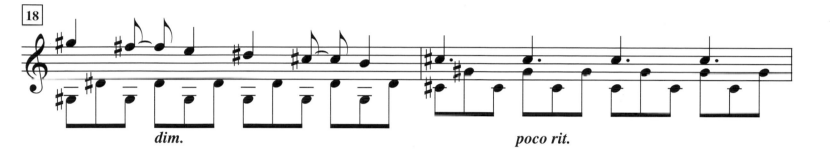

6

3 + 6

Allegro moderato (♩ = 112)

To Coda ⊕

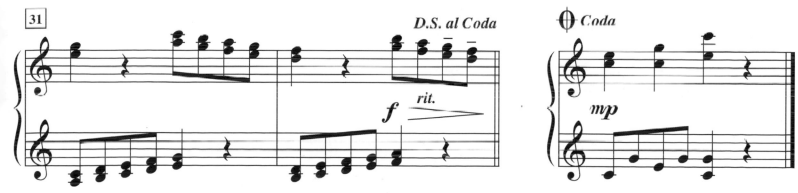

Musing

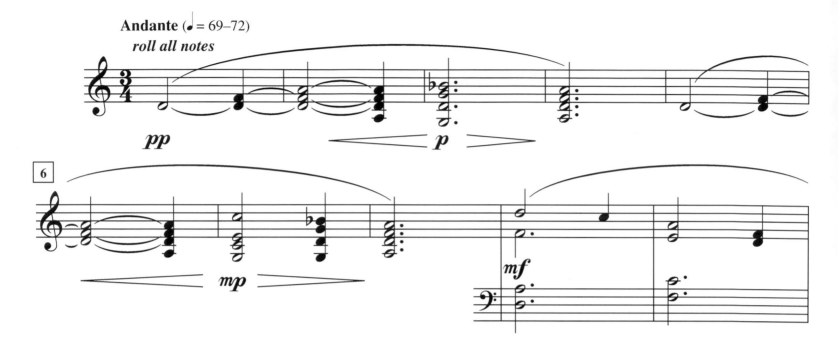

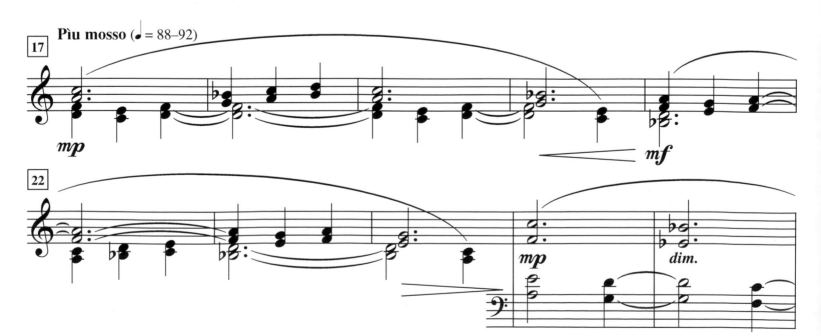

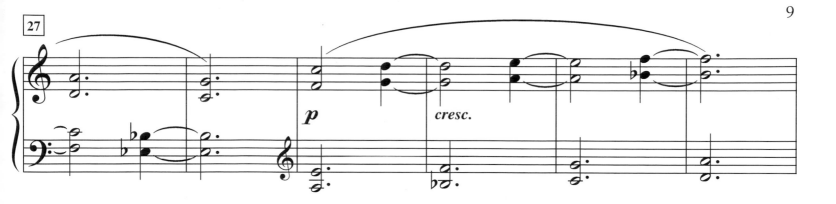

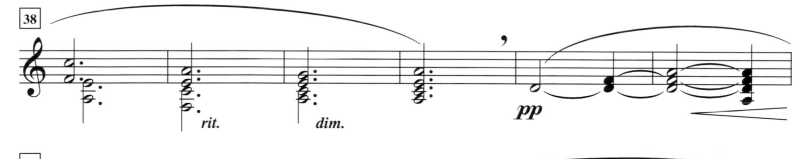

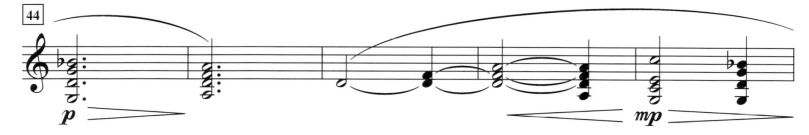

Escapade

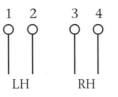

Daybreak

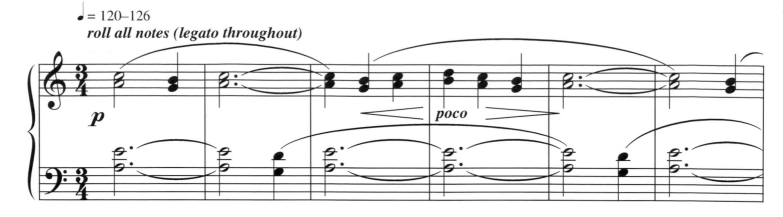

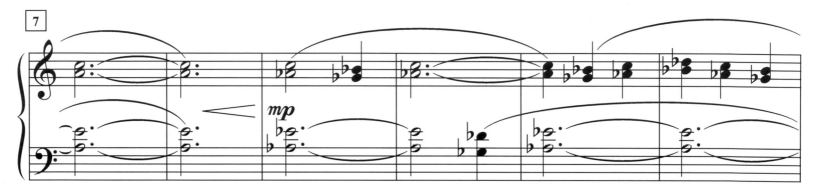

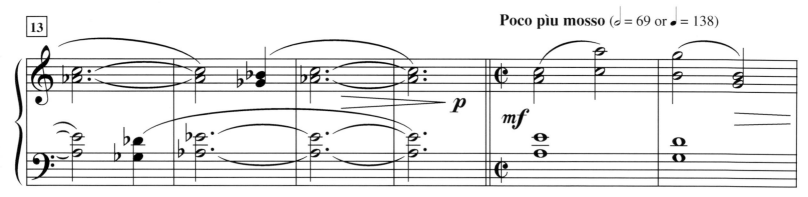

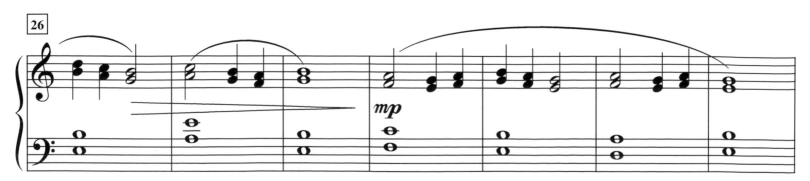

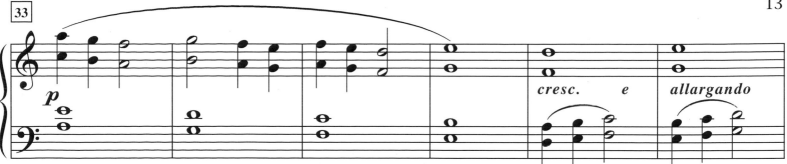

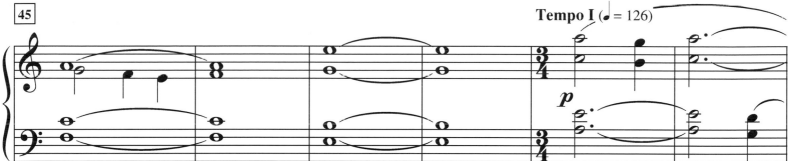

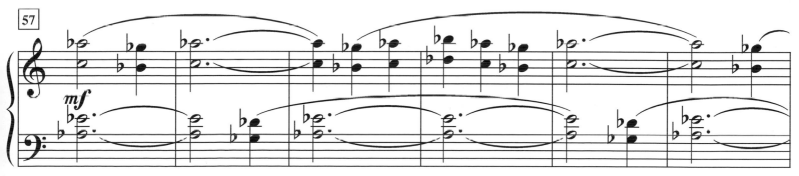

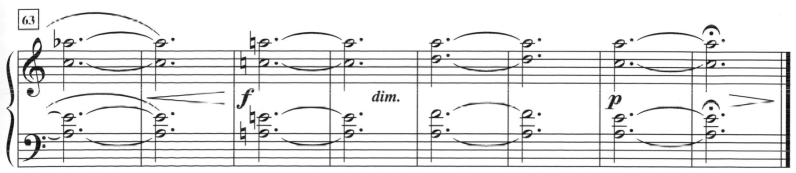

Louis Crab

Adrift

Dragonfly

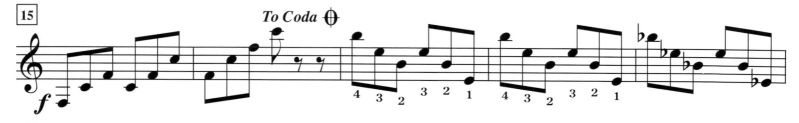

Sojourn

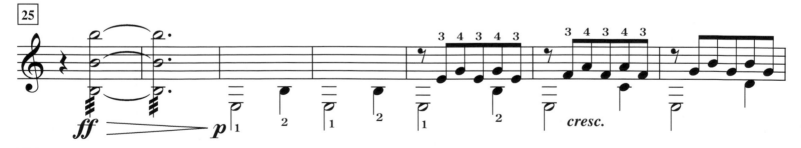

20

Chorale and Variations

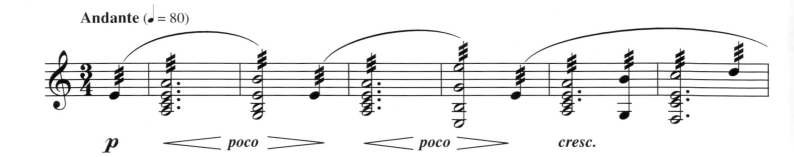

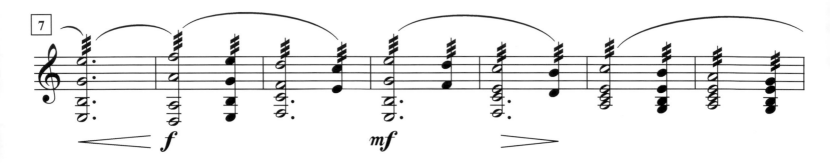

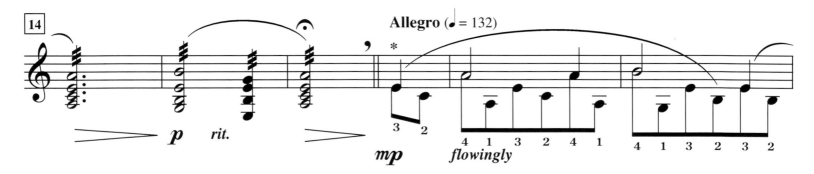

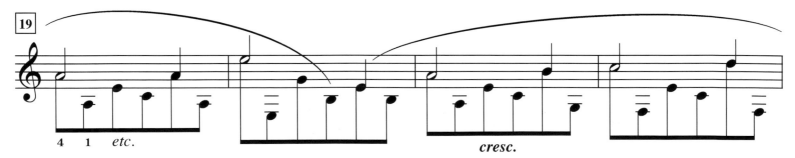

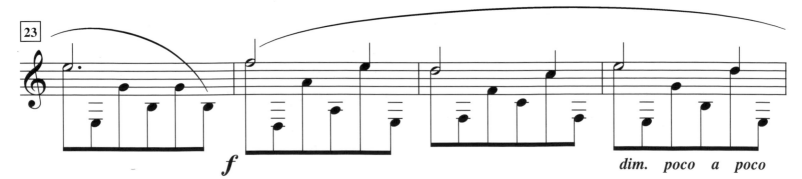

* Notes with double stems should be brought out slightly.

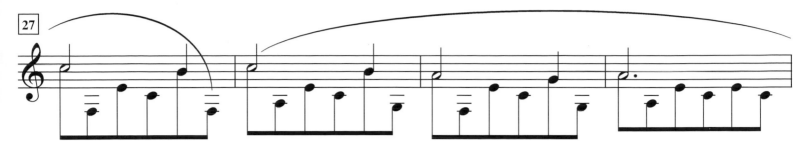

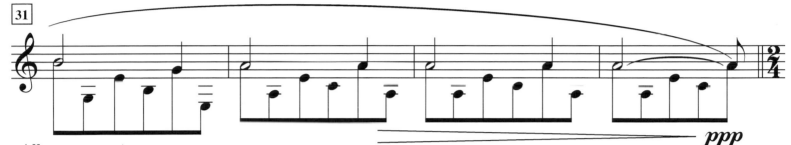

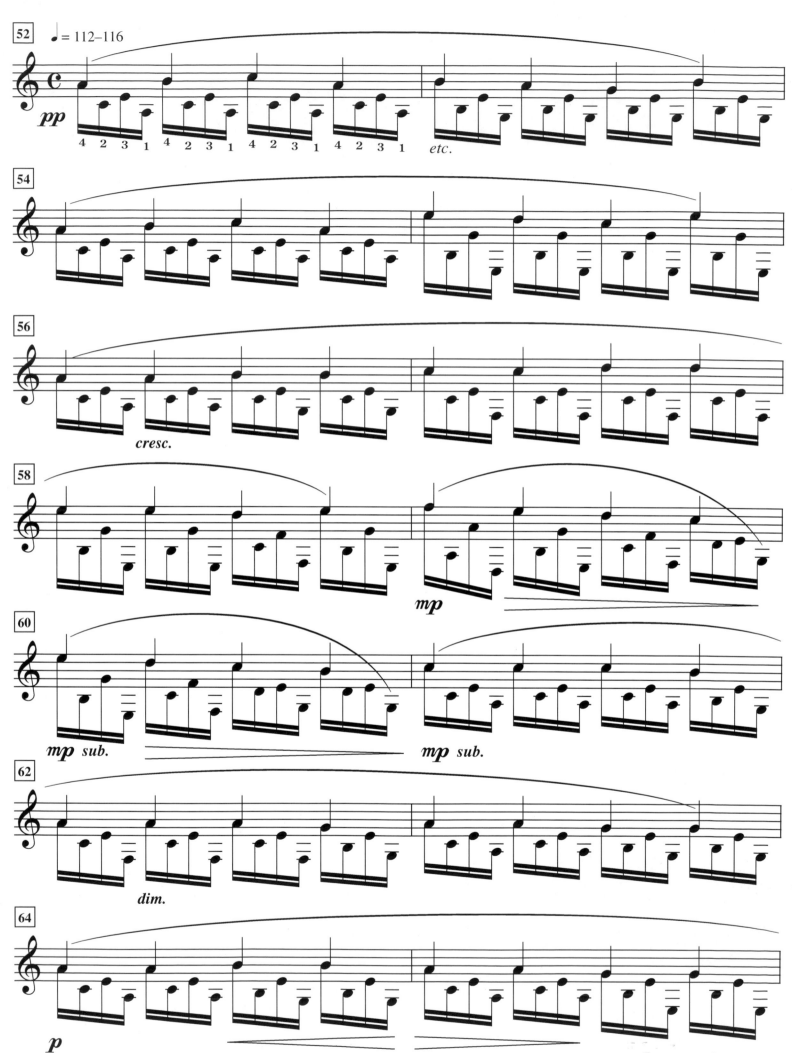

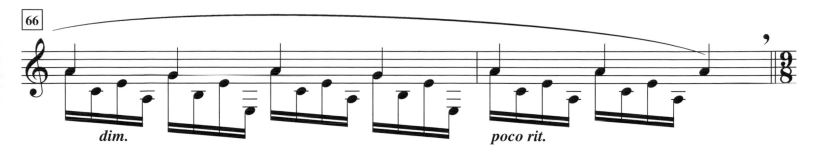

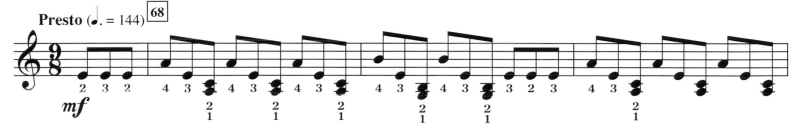